Original title:
The Porch of Memories

Copyright © 2025 Creative Arts Management OÜ
All rights reserved.

Author: Colin Harrington
ISBN HARDBACK: 978-1-80587-203-0
ISBN PAPERBACK: 978-1-80587-673-1

Reflections in the Evening Breeze

A kite got tangled in my hair,
My neighbor's laughter filled the air.
The cat stole my sandwich on the way,
As seagulls clapped for a great buffet.

We stumbled on tales of days gone by,
Belly laughs echoed as we sighed.
The fireflies danced like little stars,
While memories mingled like buzzing guitars.

Footprints in Dust and Daydreams

Sandals left tracks on the sunbaked road,
Chasing down whispers of stories owed.
A spilt drink looked like art on the floor,
We laughed till we couldn't take it anymore.

Old bikes leaned against the rusty fence,
Each pedal a giggle, and pure innocence.
Pine cones fell down with a comical thud,
While we reminisced about youthful mud.

Where Seasons Lean Against Weathered Beams

The old swing squeaked with every twist,
We joked it held secrets we dared not list.
Colors of leaves waltzed through the air,
As we forgot our troubles, both light and rare.

Rainy days brought puddles and mess,
Jumping in joy, we wore our wet dress.
As daylight faded into shades of glee,
We toasted to friendship with root beer tea.

Sipping Solitude with a Side of Reminiscence

Lemonade smiles on a sunlit day,
We chuckled at jumbled words we'd say.
Frog jumps behind a mystery green,
Making us wonder about what's unseen.

The clock ticked on, but we laughed it lost,
Trading our futures for stories tossed.
A quiet moment with a splash of cheer,
Sipping the past as the present drew near.

Past and Present Intertwined

Old shoes left to mold, as if they know,
Laughter echoes where wild daisies grow.
Grandma's tales from the rickety chair,
In my mind, she's dancing without a care.

Socks that don't match? It's a family trait,
On rainy days when we couldn't wait.
My youth on repeat, a sitcom's delight,
Reminiscing with snacks in a possible bite.

Little Moments on the Rail

On the wooden steps, we carved our names,
In the soft wax of time, we played silly games.
A bee tried to join in, lost in the buzz,
While we laughed at mishaps and found them a plus.

Our lemonade stand, it was quite a flop,
Two stuck lemons, yet we couldn't stop.
With each sip, we'd conjure bewildered faces,
Happiness lived in our quirky places.

Garden of Echoed Joys

The garden gnomes, holding secrets tight,
Despite painted smiles, they're ready to bite.
We'd sing to the weeds as they grew tall,
Claiming victory gifts in the summer's sprawl.

With worms as our friends, we'd share our tales,
And giggle through dirt as we plotted our fails.
In every petal, a tale of delight,
Each hilarious slip made the memories bright.

A Lantern's Glow in Quietude

A flickering glow in the evening's hush,
As we crafted shadows with laughter's rush.
Counting fireflies as they danced through the night,
While the stars chuckled down in sheer delight.

In the nighttime stillness, a joke took flight,
With crickets chirping their comedic bite.
Our giggles soared high, lighting up the sky,
In a world where the silly never says goodbye.

Gaze Beyond the Fading Horizon

On a bench where sunlight spills,
I recall those grape-stomping thrills.
Wobbly feet in sticky boots,
We laughed till snorts came in cahoots.

Old dreams dance like shadows bright,
Chasing fireflies in the night.
Each tale a treasure, not quite true,
Like the dog that stole my favorite shoe.

The wind whispers careless sighs,
As I check for those muddy ties.
Funny how time plays tricks so sly,
Was that a cat, or did I just spy?

Crickets' Tune and Heartfelt Stories

Crickets chirp their nightly song,
Under stars where we belong.
With soda pop and sticky hands,
We spun tall tales on shifting sands.

A juggling act with crowns of leaves,
Who knew laughter could deceive?
That aimless toss at grandma's cat,
I swear it looked just like a hat!

Mom's pot roast, a smoky treat,
With flavors that can't be beat.
Yet somehow, we all went 'oops!'
As dad fell headfirst in the soups.

Anchored in the Past

With flip-flops on, we race the tide,
Chasing memories, wide-eyed, spry.
A pirate ship made from driftwood,
Where sails were dreams, mischief we brewed.

Grandpa's stories of days gone by,
How he once flew—almost hit the sky!
A paper plane, with curvy flight,
We laughed till dawn chased away the night.

But every joke has its own cost,
Like that time we thought we'd be lost.
Maps we scribbled, quite the art,
Leading us right back to the start.

A Seat Among the Stars

In starry nights we spread our schemes,
Swapping silly, wild dreams.
With popcorn bowls and wobbly chairs,
We ventured deep into the dares.

Aliens called, gave me a fright,
Did we just fall? No, it's all right!
An interstellar trip, on a whim,
With laughter that would never dim.

The universe, a playground vast,
Where sing-alongs are built to last.
Yet in the end, what's truly right,
Is everything's better shared at night.

Unraveled Threads of Lived Moments

Worn-out shoes stacked up high,
Each pair tells a tale, oh my!
A squirrel once stole my sandwich,
It ran off with such a bandage.

Naps on chairs that creak and sigh,
Bugs buzzing all around me fly.
I waved at a cloud, it ignored my cheer,
Guess humor's lost to nostrils here.

Rustic Reveries Under the Open Sky

A cat sprawls where the daisies grow,
It dreams of mice that dare to show.
Two chickens gossip, pecking round,
While the broom lies lost and found.

The sunbeams dance with charming flair,
A hat flies off—a windblown scare!
We laugh at shadows, stretching wide,
As squirrels plot their great nutty tide.

Heartbeats in the Silence of Dusk

Fireflies flicker in a waltz,
Each glimmer hides why we halt.
An old radio sings tunes out of tune,
We hum along, a silly boon.

Crickets click with a cheeky beat,
While ants parade, oh, so elite.
With each puff of passing breeze,
Time tickles us with such ease.

Tattered Quilts of Time and Treasures

Old photos tangled in a box,
I find the one where Dad wore socks.
The quilt is frayed, but the tales are bright,
Of family feasts gone well by night.

Whiskers on a laughing face,
Grandma's recipes—oh, what a race!
"Too much sugar," she would chide,
Yet sweetened chaos swelled with pride.

Sun-Kissed Hours and Silent Soliloquies

The sun slouched low, a lazy cat,
Laughing at thoughts in a floppy hat.
Sipping lemonade, I squint and sigh,
As bees argue over who gets the pie.

Old chairs creak like a comedy play,
While kids race by, in a lively ballet.
My neighbor sneezes, it's quite a scene,
In this sun-soaked nook, all feels serene.

A squirrel steals a sandwich, oh what a theft!
Chasing his shadow, he's quite the chef.
Time drips like honey, sticky and sweet,
Each laugh a reminder, a playful repeat.

Wearily, cats nap on the fence post,
In dreams of fish, they laugh and boast.
As day dims down, the giggles stay bright,
In this silly world, everything feels right.

Memories Settled Like Dust on the Rail

Dust bunnies dance, they're having a ball,
An invite to join? I might take that call.
Old toys lie scattered like scattered thoughts,
Each rusting treasure my memory haunts.

Worn-out shoes tell stories of leaps,
While pigeons scold me for losing my peeps.
They're plotting to steal my last few fries,
With their beady eyes full of mischief and lies.

The swing creaks softly, shadows move slow,
I try to recall the last time it snowed.
But laughter escapes like a runaway kite,
Tangled in whispers, everything feels light.

Amidst all the chaos, I sip from my cup,
Forgetting my worries, I let my heart up.
With dust settled nicely, I'm ready to play,
In this recollection, oh what a day!

Fleeting Hues of a Daydream's Edge

Colors swirl wildly, like ice cream gone rogue,
I chase after giggles that come from the fog.
A butterfly teases with a flitty dance,
While I trip over memories in a silly trance.

The hammock sways with gossipy tales,
Of how birds gossip and how laughter never fails.
Time takes a tumble, trying to keep up,
With the sights of old friends and half-empty cups.

Clouds morph into shapes, a dog or a shoe,
Each glimpse a giggle, what a view!
I laugh as a breeze tickles my nose,
And hear echoes of joy blowing where it goes.

Daylight tightropes on laughter's thin thread,
As the sun paints dreams in hues of red.
In moments of madness under the sky's edge,
I tiptoe on whimsy, I happily pledge.

Beneath the Stars, Where Dreams Spoke Softly

Stars wink down, twinkling in play,
Whispers float by, mischievous ballet.
A marshmallow roast, sticks poised with cheer,
While dreams giggle softly, pulling me near.

Fireflies tango like stars made of light,
Each flicker a smile buried deep in the night.
I try to catch one, but they giggle and dart,
Echoing secrets that tickle my heart.

The moon is a jester, grinning so wide,
It teases the shadows that lurk at its side.
Jokes roll like tumbleweeds, wild and free,
As laughter takes flight on the breeze with glee.

With the night painting tales with a twist,
I swing in the laughter, impossible to miss.
Under this canopy, my heart takes control,
In the silliness woven, I find my soul.

Gentle Tides of Remembrance

Sipping lemonade, we laugh out loud,
Echoes of laughter from the crowd.
Mismatched stories float like clouds,
As we reminisce about the proud.

Grandma's wig fell into the pie,
We laughed so hard, I thought I'd cry.
Her cat wore it, oh my, oh my,
Now every feast feels like a fry.

Old photos hide in a dusty chest,
With silly faces, we look our best.
The dance moves? A mediocre quest,
Yet in our hearts, we feel so blessed.

Time is a thief that steals the days,
But in these tales, our spirit plays.
Each chuckle comes in unexpected ways,
As joy and laughter fill the bays.

The Sway of Nostalgia

Swinging in chairs where secrets bloom,
Frogs in the night croon their tune.
A cat walks by, eyeing my broom,
And I swear it thinks it can zoom.

We swapped our cookies for candy bars,
Dropped our ice cream while counting stars.
Told ghost stories with twisted cars,
Until we laughed, had fallen hard.

The neighbor's dog stole Uncle Fred's hat,
Now it's a trophy, not just a spat.
We cheered it on, oh, imagine that,
As it pranced away, proud as a brat.

Old records spin with a crackle and pop,
Dancing like robots, we can't stop.
If memories fade, we'll just hop,
To that rhythm where giggles drop.

Lost in the Lull of Evening

As the sun dips, shadows grow tall,
We recall the time our car hit a wall.
Dad said it wasn't a crash at all,
Just a gentle nudge, a friendly call.

The fireflies join our little show,
With stories of stumbles, slip-ups in tow.
Mom's dancing style? A classic faux,
But that's the charm we all know.

The stars blink down with mischief and glee,
Whispering tales of old family spree.
If laughter could echo, how loud would it be?
In our hearts, it twinkles, eternally free.

Evening wraps us in a comfy embrace,
With goofy grins on every face.
In this lull, our memories race,
Funny moments feel like a warm place.

Fragments of a Woven Tale

Threads of laughter weave through the air,
Mom's burnt toast? Always beyond compare.
Recipes gone rogue, who really dares?
Yet we feast on joy, no room for despair.

Crazy hats made from things around,
Dancing like nobody's on solid ground.
Pranks staged cleverly, what madness found,
The bonds grow stronger, memory-bound.

Uncles recite tales that twist and turn,
Of mishaps that spark and brightly burn.
Like a game of charades, we hilariously learn,
That in our chaos, friendships discern.

Even as time trickles like sand,
These moments are golden, never bland.
In our woven tale, we proudly stand,
With laughter's thread tightly in hand.

Fleeting Glimpses of Time

On a chair that squeaks and groans,
Old stories dance like wayward drones.
A teacup slips, the cat leaps high,
While I just chuckle, oh my, oh my!

Nostalgia rolls in like a summer breeze,
Mixing laughter with old memories with ease.
A bird that wanders too close to snack,
Pokes fun at me, then makes a swift back.

Grandpa's hat hangs, oh what a sight,
Sitting askew, it's a comical plight.
He wears his wisdom like a funny shawl,
Every shared joke, it ticks like a ball.

As shadows stretch across the grass,
Across the years, we'll let them pass.
With every chuckle that slips through the air,
Life's little quirks, we're all just a pair!

Sunlit Shadows of Reflection

Sunbeams tease through the swaying trees,
An old horse neighs at the buzzing bees.
We slip on laughter, trip on the rug,
Sharing tales that make us feel snug.

Old sneakers toss in the gentle light,
Each crease a laugh from yesterday's fight.
Memories swirl in a dance with the wind,
Tickling the heart where the laughter's pinned.

Lost in the stories, we sometimes beg,
Is that the dog or some neighbor's leg?
With fuzzy tales and a can of soda,
Life's odd moments should win a supernova.

As shadows of sunlight play tag at noon,
We dance with echoes, a silly tune.
Cackles and snorts mark the day we keep,
Replaying the laughter that never does sleep!

Threads of Silver in the Fabric of Days

In the sewing box lies laughter's thread,
Mom's patchwork wisdom, brightly spread.
Poking through with a needle of fun,
Stitching memories, one by one.

A button misplaced in a laughter spree,
As it rolls away, can it catch the bee?
Fumbled stories, winding like twine,
Each twist and turn a memory divine.

Sunset hues flicker in wobbly chairs,
As we spill secrets over the night air.
With popcorn tales from the distant past,
The best of times, we hold them fast.

So where's that sock? Oh, let it be,
Under a mound of sweet jubilee.
Laughter lingers and stitches so tight,
Through threads of silver, we welcome the night!

A Window to What Was

In the corner sits a chair,
Faded fabric, a bit of wear.
Stories told with laughter bright,
Ghosts of jokes that took to flight.

A cat that knows too much, it seems,
Chasing shadows, killing dreams.
We recall the friends that strayed,
And laughter's echo that delayed.

Grandma's cookies left their mark,
While grandpa danced with silly spark.
Spilled secrets, mustard stains,
Tickled hearts with funny gains.

So many moments wrapped in grace,
In this cozy, silly space.
A window to the past we hold,
Through laughter, tales of old retold.

The Sound of Silence and Sighs

The clock ticks loud, just like my cat,
Who ponders life like an old diplomat.
Muffled giggles hid from view,
As dusty shadows dance anew.

In quiet terms, we often muse,
About those times we'd gladly choose.
A broken teacup speaks of fun,
As memories race beneath the sun.

We sigh not deep but lightly so,
Thinking of where those giggles go.
In silence shared like secret code,
We hunt the laughter's hidden load.

Yet echoes come of what we've lost,
In whispers sweet, they count the cost.
Each sigh a bridge to joyful tales,
Where laughter lingers, love prevails.

Solitude Wrapped in Warmth

A cup of cocoa, warm and sweet,
Melting memories, a little treat.
In solitude, I find my fun,
A jester's cap when day is done.

Comfy socks with silly prints,
Chasing laughter, teasing hints.
Here I sit, with shadows play,
Where solitude meets a joke's delay.

The world outside can bounce and reel,
While here, each silly thought I feel.
A solo dance, a quirky spin,
Pajama days where joys begin.

I wear my solitude with pride,
In giggles, I can now confide.
Wrapped in warmth of funny dreams,
The laughter flows in silly streams.

Crossroads of Light and Shadow

A light bulb flickers, just for fun,
Casting shadows as day is done.
Between the lanes of laugh and cry,
A memory flutters, passing by.

Two paths diverge, one dull, one bright,
Where jokes were traded, day and night.
Here lies the land of mix-up tales,
Where humor sets its vibrant sails.

Old albums hide beneath the stairs,
Full of faces, giggles, and glares.
As sunlight spills on open space,
Laughter paints a silly face.

At this crossroads, we find our way,
Through laughter's tune, we choose to play.
Light and shadow dance and weave,
In every memory, we believe.

Days Spent in Golden Sunbeams

In the backyard, we'd often meet,
Sipping lemonade, oh what a treat!
The cat lounged with effortless grace,
While ants marched on a culinary race.

We'd share stories of daring feats,
Like the time you danced on your two left feet.
The sun painted our laughter in gold,
As we plotted new adventures bold.

With grass stains and sticky hands,
We built castles from old rubber bands.
And as the day turned into night,
We laughed till our smiles felt just right.

Conversations with the Stars

On summer nights, we'd gaze up high,
Inventing tales of the moon's sly eye.
"Is that a comet or just a plane?"
You'd argue with me again and again.

The stars winked as if they'd heard,
Every silly, nonsensical word.
We debated if aliens might land,
While lying on the soft, cool sand.

You swore one twinkled just for you,
I claimed it sent me secrets too.
We found constellations in warming beams,
And turned our dreams into wild schemes.

Stitched Together by Time

In grandma's quilt, we'd share our dreams,
Piecing together life's funny themes.
You'd point out the squares, how they wrinkled,
Each one a tale, like a star just twinkled.

We stitched laughter in colors so bright,
Knitted moments that felt just right.
The threads of mischief, the yarns of glee,
Woven with love, forever carefree.

We'd argue over whose square was best,
While the quilt embraced us like a nest.
Every patch held secrets, stories to tell,
Like why you thought jellybeans rang the bell.

Footsteps in Starlight

We danced in shadows when dusk arrived,
Chasing fireflies, we felt so alive.
The grass tickled our toes in delight,
As laughter echoed through the night.

You once tripped over a root on the way,
And ended up laughing the night away.
With footsteps echoing soft as a sigh,
We chased after dreams like birds in the sky.

Each star was a wish that we'd toss and roll,
Turning our mischief into playful soul.
We left our footprints on the moonlit lane,
Stories of starlight, never mundane.

Twilight Conversations with Ghosts of Youth

In twilight's glow, we laugh and tease,
Reliving moments with youthful ease.
Silly tales of things we wore,
Like mismatched socks and dance on the floor.

A blanket fort made of couch and sheets,
Where victories were won with imaginary feats.
We spoke of love, and then forgot,
Who had a crush on whom? Now who cares a lot!

Old toys whisper secrets, oh so bold,
Plastic soldiers guarding treasures of gold.
Those ghostly figures dance in delight,
While we debate who had the best ice cream bite!

As evening wraps its gentle arms,
We share our childhood silly charms.
A hefty dose of laughter, we sow,
In twilight's embrace, we steal the show.

Rustling Leaves and Faded Greetings

Beneath the trees, we gather round,
Whispers of laughter in rustling sound.
'Remember that time we rode a kite?'
Flying too high, what a silly sight!

The leaves chuckle, they know it well,
How we stumbled, tripped, and fell.
Our fading greetings like echoes play,
In colors of laughter, we sway and sway.

With cookie crumbs stuck to our shirts,
Sharing old dances, oh how it flirts.
We spin and twirl in life's gentle breeze,
In rustling leaves, we find our ease.

The fading sun winks at our fun,
As stories wrap up, one by one.
In a golden hue, the past we greet,
With rustling leaves beneath our feet.

Gaze Beyond the Quirks of the Past

Come sit with me, let's have a laugh,
Remember the time we tried to gaff?
A cactus dressed for our school play,
   Twirling about in a prickly ballet!

Images swirl like a merry-go-round,
Each quirk a treasure that we have found.
From clashing shirts to shoe-laced fights,
Gazing back brings those silly delights.

There's magic in stories, and more to be told,
 Of brave little knights, and pretend gold.
  The quirks of the past are our delight,
    Laughter echoing into the night.

So let's raise a toast to those wild days,
With goofy grins and spontaneous plays.
 In stories shared, we surely will bask,
   Gazing beyond, that's all I ask!

Gathering of Traces in Twilight's Glow

In twilight's glow, we gather near,
With traces of laughter and a glass of cheer.
Old photographs telling tales unsaid,
Of circus dreams and pillow fights in bed.

Giggles erupt from dusty shelves,
As we recount the tales of our youthful elves.
A time when the world was our playground wide,
And pigeons were dragons we feared to ride!

Collecting our remnants like firefly glow,
From epic quests to the friends we know.
With every voice, the past comes alive,
In this gathering, our spirits thrive.

So here we are, in laughter we bathe,
With wild imaginations that we still save.
Twilight hugs us as night begins to flow,
In this gathering of traces, we brightly glow.

Unwinding Stories of Knots and Twine

In a corner sits a chair,
With stories wrapped in flair.
Old socks and tied-up shoes,
Waiting for the nightly news.

A cat that swears it's a dog,
Chasing shadows through the fog.
A teapot whistling tunes of old,
While laughter hangs, warm and bold.

Grandpa's tales of quirky pranks,
Make us all break into ranks.
A rubber band that once was grand,
Now just stretches, lost its brand.

As we sip our lemonade,
Memories dance, never fade.
With knots and twine, we're intertwined,
Creating chaos, fully signed.

Pebbles Remembering the Footsteps

Pebbles scatter on the ground,
Each one hides a tale unbound.
Carried by shoes that kick and scuff,
Remember when the road got tough?

Mismatched socks on laundry day,
Daring shoes to run away.
Bouncing rocks with stories tight,
Wondering if we'll return tonight.

Tiptoe whispers on the street,
Giggles echo, oh so sweet.
Every pebble's got a knack,
For remembering the silly track.

As night falls, the stories lay,
In every stone, a fun display.
With footsteps trapped in stone so fine,
We dance again, age doesn't confine.

Fragments of Heartbeats in Wooden Cracks

Old floorboards creak with glee,
Whispering secrets just for me.
A ghost of laughter skips around,
In echoes of the past, we're found.

Wooden cracks like tiny seams,
Holding all our silly dreams.
From travel tales and jumped-up pies,
To midnight snacks and starlit skies.

Grandma's chair that squeaks so loud,
Holds all the joy; it's quite proud.
Each heartbeat's rhythm fills the air,
In fragments shared, we all declare.

So sit awhile, don't rush away,
Let laughter guide the night to play.
In these cracks, we find our tunes,
In wooden grooves beneath the moon.

Songs of Yesterday in Gentle Breezes

Soft whispers ride the evening air,
Songs of yesteryear, lively fare.
A breeze that dances through the trees,
Tickling secrets, jumping knees.

Chasing fireflies, we'll sing out loud,
Covering mischief in a shroud.
Old records scratch, but we don't care,
Life's a joke we joyfully share.

Windy tales of ice cream drips,
And how we always lose our chips.
The song of laughter floats around,
With every note, a joy profound.

As night wraps us in velvet grace,
We find our rhythm, we find our place.
In gentle breezes, we shall hum,
To sweet nostalgia, we always come.

Wishes Laid upon the Rail

A squirrel stole my sandwich, quite a twist,
I chased him down, but he was too brisk.
He winked at me with a twitch of his tail,
And I laughed so hard, forgot my own fail.

Old shoes hung high like ghosts in the air,
Each pair told stories of journeys rare.
I swear one squeaked out a joke on the line,
It tickled my heart, a soft laugh divine.

The wind whispered secrets with a cheeky tune,
As a cat lazed around, snoozing by noon.
It dreamt of fish in a bowl made of glass,
While I plotted to catch it, a scheme made to pass.

Cousin Fred showed up with a hair so wild,
Declared himself a rock star, but we just smiled.
He strummed on a broom and sang a new song,
We applauded his efforts, where did we go wrong?

Memories on the Dusk's Breath

Bubbles in the twilight, oh what a sight,
A kid with a wand, and pure sheer delight.
They floated like dreams, then popped with a cheer,
I caught one in laughter; it just wouldn't steer.

Uncle Joe came bearing gifts of old bites,
He warned us of monsters that haunt on cold nights.
With every tall tale, we'd laugh and we'd moan,
While Grandma rolled her eyes, her humor well-known.

A raccoon scuffled by with mischief in mind,
He swiped all our snacks, never caring, unkind.
We dealt with the chaos, our giggles would swell,
In a world where he conquered, the king of the knell.

Candles flickered softly, then snuffed with a breath,
While laughter lingered on, there was no hint of death.
We toasted to years filled with whimsy and cheer,
With a wink to the moon, as memories drew near.

Bygone Days and Lantern Glow

The lanterns flickered, casting shadows so bold,
While we chased down stories from days long told.
A game of tag broke out, like whispers in air,
While dogs joined the chase, without any care.

Nana would chuckle, recounting her dreams,
Of dancing with pirates and savoring creams.
Her wisdom was funny, with a wink and a grin,
As she topped her tall tale with a dusting of sin.

We built a small fort from old garden chairs,
And ruled as young kings, with grand regal airs.
Each cushion, a throne, each pillow, a fight,
Defending our kingdom till lost in the night.

Then slipped off to sleep as stars twinkled bright,
In a realm filled with giggles that danced in the night.
Tomorrow would greet us with more to unleash,
To welcome new memories, and laughter's sweet feast.

Bridge to the Heart's Echo

We crossed a bridge made of old wooden planks,
Each step creaked a story, and earned our thanks.
With a goat on the bank, munching away,
He nodded in wisdom, perhaps he would stay.

Lemonade stains on this porch, so divine,
We made it a sport, a summertime shrine.
With sticky fingers and grins wide as the sun,
We laughed till our faces, were virtually one.

The garden gnomes grinned, their stash hidden well,
Full of secrets and stories, they had much to tell.
We leaned in close, with a giggle and hush,
As they whispered the tricks for a prankish rush.

When evenings fell softly with crickets on song,
We sang to the stars, where we all still belong.
The memories linger like fireflies aglow,
In a place built of laughter, where hearts come and go.

Layers of a Life Lived

Stacked high like old newspapers,
Each layer holds a tale,
The cat's still eyeing the pizza,
As we sip drinks without fail.

Memory's like a wet sponge,
Soak it in, let it leak,
A sneeze at the wrong moment,
Might unleash another peek!

Jokes told in hushed whispers,
Echo loud through the haze,
Each laugh like a firecracker,
A burst in our playful days.

With each silly mishap,
We learn not to take flight,
For the layers we pile up,
Are our anchors, not our plight.

Remnants of Laughter in the Air

Squeaky swings played our song,
As we whizzed through the day,
Spilled juice and ticklish toes,
In a most peculiar way.

Echoes of grandma's chuckles,
Dance in the afternoon light,
Her wig flew off in a gust,
Now that's a comical sight!

Kites tangled 'round tree branches,
Becoming the ultimate prank,
Who knew childhood mischief,
Could bring us such a rank?

From silly sayings to grand falls,
Our stories are never bare,
For every giggle remains,
As remnants in the air.

The Gentle Rocking of Time

On a swing, we sway slowly,
As tales bubble up from below,
Old socks in mismatched glory,
Worn pride that steals the show.

Time rocks like a cradle,
With laughter stitched through the seams,
Grandpa's jokes still echo,
In the midst of our wild dreams.

Each dent tells a different story,
Every creak is a friend,
As humor becomes timeless,
When we each take a blend.

So let's sit back and chuckle,
As the world twirls and spins,
In this rocking chair of life,
The funny never thins.

Faded Photos on the Railing

Photos flutter in the breeze,
Captured mishaps and more,
Each snapshot a moment,
Our lives a comedy store.

A pie on the face of the uncle,
That camping trip gone wrong,
We laugh 'til our sides ache,
In our never-ending song.

Children dancing in the rain,
Wearing buckets as hats,
Memories bright as fireworks,
Our time's a party of spats.

So here's to those faded frames,
Hanging on the old railing,
In every smile, a reminder,
Of laughter never failing.

The Magic of Unspoken Words

In whispers soft like winter's breath,
We dance around what's never said.
A nod, a wink, a chuckle shared,
In silence, laughter's easily spread.

The cat's on the roof, a king on high,
While grandpa sneezes, the dogwaves bye.
A secret joke held tight in a grin,
What joy it is, the games we spin!

With every glance, a tale unfolds,
Of chocolate stains and pranks of old.
A silent shout, a giggle snored,
We build our stories, wordless, adored.

Oh how we bumble through the day,
With funny tales tucked safely away.
A shared idea that clicks so well,
In this laughter fuelled spell we dwell.

Memories Like Autumn Leaves

The crunch beneath our eager feet,
A pile of leaves, a grand retreat.
We leap, we twirl, we giggle loud,
In splendid chaos, joy's our shroud.

Uncle's hat, a silly sight,
He struts about, pure delight.
The leaves they swirl, the laughter rings,
As mischief dances on fallen wings.

The dog's a blur in shades of brown,
While grandma laughs, her words a crown.
She tells of days in the yellow sun,
When life's own games were all in fun.

With every gust, a tale takes flight,
Memories spun in golden light.
Who knew that leaves could hold such cheer,
In breezy whispers, love draws near.

Sipping Tea with Shadows

In the corner, shadows sway,
As tea leaves spin and dance away.
A splash of lemon, a hint of cheer,
Two mugs clink in the fading year.

A grandpa's tale upturned the cup,
Of toe-nail clippings finding luck.
We sip and grin, a warm delight,
As stories sip into the night.

With every slurp, a chuckle flows,
While grandma stirs her sugar woes.
The crumbs of biscuits scatter wide,
As laughter spills, we cannot hide.

The shadows pull their ancient games,
They dance with glee, they share our names.
Sipping tea, we hold them tight,
In every shadow, warmth takes flight.

Echoes in the Twilight Breeze

As twilight stretches, shadows play,
A dance of echoes at the end of day.
With fireflies shining like stars unspooled,
We laugh at stories, zany and ruled.

A tree that bends, the wise old sage,
Whispers secrets from a forgotten page.
A squirrel pauses, a puzzled frown,
At tales of socks and the mystery brown.

The breeze brings whispers of childish fun,
Of cream pies thrown and races run.
We point and giggle at past misdeeds,
In shadows bold, our laughter leads.

Through echoes we hear our voices blend,
In twilight's grasp, all troubles mend.
With every chuckle, our hearts now wave,
In the gentle breeze, memories brave.

Storyteller's Corner on the Steps

On the steps where tales unfold,
Laughing echoes, bright and bold.
Mismatched socks and missing shoes,
These are the stories we choose.

Grandpa's jokes, a little twisted,
About the cat that never existed.
We all chime in with our parts,
Crafting laughter, winning hearts.

Milk spills and puns that stick,
The garden gnome, a clever trick.
Old dog snores, sprawled on the floor,
In shade of memories, we want more.

Warm Embrace of Yesterday

Silly hats from a bygone day,
Danced around in such a way.
Each mismatched mitten, full of cheer,
Worn by wishes, never fear.

We'll share a secret for the best,
How crayons can turn into a guest.
Laugh lines deep, like canyon trails,
Memories float on giggling gales.

Games of tag with rules quite vague,
Use sticks as swords, or a leafy plague.
The neighbors peeked, what a sight,
Laughter carried into the night.

Whispers of What Was

In corner nooks where whispers sway,
We spin our dreams as night turns day.
A laundry basket full of cheer,
Who knew socks could disappear?

Racing bikes down mystery lanes,
Trying to dodge the raindrop trains.
Chasing shadows in the sun,
Every mischief—so much fun!

Dandelions in a crown of glee,
The world is ours! Just you and me.
We count the clouds, a fluffy fleet,
With giggles stuck to our bare feet.

Imprints of Joyful Laughter

Footprints zigzag on the floor,
Sponge cake crumbs? Oh, just a score.
Playful banter, a cookie raid,
Let's hope the last one hasn't faded!

Tile by tile, we sketch our fun,
Juggling sunshine, toss and run!
An acorn hat perched on a head,
Why be normal? Let's be led!

Spinning tales of clumsy grace,
Ice cream drips, a sticky race.
Life's sweet scoop, a funny flavor,
In every laugh, we find our savior.

Shadows on the Wooden Steps

Frog jumped high, landed with a plop,
Old cat watching, thinking, "Stop!"
Neighbors whisper tales of the moon,
While my old shoe squeaks in tune.

Squirrel steals nuts, dances with glee,
Chasing shadows, oh look at me!
Dog barks loudly at a passing leaf,
As I chuckle, can't help but grieve.

Time ticks on, but laughter stays,
Each creak a reminder of funny days.
With every step on these aged planks,
Memories spring forth, no need for thanks.

So here's to life on these wooden steps,
Where every bump gives us more prep.
Be it a dance or a silly smile,
We gather our joy, and stay awhile.

Reflections in the Evening Glow

As dusk settles, the shadows creep,
The goldfish dreams, but does not sleep.
Neighbors dispute who had the loudest snack,
While I reminisce on my great hat rack.

Sunset paints with comedic flair,
The dog prances as if in midair.
Uncle Joe's belly laughs like thunder,
While Aunt Mabel rolls her eyes in wonder.

Old jokes revive in the fading light,
Like old moths trying to take their flight.
The swing creaks with memories' echo,
As laughter dances in evening's glow.

So raise a toast to those who laugh,
And let each story be our photograph.
In this glow, we share our delight,
With every chuckle, our hearts feel light.

Stories Woven in Dust

Amidst the dust, tall tales emerge,
Of that cat who thought he could purge.
Grandma's knitting, but yarn goes astray,
Each stitch visits a comic ballet.

Dust motes swirl like whispers bright,
Of socks lost in the laundry fight.
Timmy's big splashes, the water flew,
Mom's quick cover, what's a kid to do?

In absence of a grand tale's grace,
A tumble, a trip—what a funny place!
The stories rise, like clouds on high,
In giggles and grins that never die.

So, here's to dust and tales that spin,
Each memory twinkling, where we've been.
Laughing 'til the sun fades away,
These woven stories, our hearts will play.

Sunbeams and Soft Goodbyes

Sunbeams dance on the faded chairs,
While laughter sings through the warm summer air.
Goodbyes are just excuses to tease,
As friends pull pranks with the greatest of ease.

Each smile a reminder, each joke a clue,
Of wild adventures that always ensue.
Weighing each step on the path of time,
With memories flavored with soft lime.

Mom's lemonade, as sweet as her grin,
Filled with laughter and tales to spin.
Leaving feels funny, as echoes still chime,
In each soft goodbye, we grab for more time.

Sunsets turn gold, and shadows sway,
With chuckles that linger, they hang and play.
So let's raise our glasses and laugh one more round,
In this symphony where joy's always found.

Porch Swing Lullabies to Past Reflections

Rocking back and forth in time,
We laugh at our youthful grime.
Each creak a chuckle, each sway a tease,
As we recall our silly misdeeds.

A lemonade spill, a pet cat's chase,
Chasing a ghost in a paper-thin space.
Skipping stones, we were kings of the day,
With crown made of dandelions, hip-hip-hooray!

A neighbor's wig blew into our yard,
We wore it proudly, it wasn't that hard!
The gossip flew faster than a dove,
Though I can't say it fit like a glove.

Now we sit, and the swing does slow,
With memories that dance like a glowing show.
We chuckle at moments that gave us delight,
These lullabies wrapped in the soft twilight.

Lantern Light on Forgotten Faces

Beneath flickering light, old friends gather near,
Sharing tales over popcorn and old root beer.
The shadows play tricks, putting on quite a show,
As we recall the times when we stole the dough.

The night we thought we'd fly like the birds,
But only fell flat, in a sea of words.
With a sigh and a giggle, we shrug off the fright,
Oh, how we stumbled under the moonlight!

The lantern sways gentle, casting silly grins,
While we relive the antics of our childish sins.
One wore mismatched socks, one wore a bright hat,
We looked like something straight out of a mat!

So here we are, in a whirl of delight,
Under lanterns, our past shines bright.
With laughter and chuckles, we raise a toast,
To memories and mishaps that matter the most.

Whispers of Forgotten Days

The wind speaks softly, a cheeky tease,
Bringing back days with such playful ease.
We built our dreams in a fort of sheets,
And played silly games on our own two feet.

There's a tale of a frog, a prince in disguise,
Who made quite the splash, oh, what a surprise!
With each little song and the tattle of toes,
We danced through the grass where adventure arose.

Now we sit shaded by bones of the past,
Waving goodbye to the darkness so vast.
With whispers of pink clouds ticking along,
The echoes of giggles like a sweet, silly song.

So raise up your glass, to the moments we've won,
To laughter and joy, let's party till done.
For life is a garden, we tend it with care,
Sprinkled with laughter and loving to share.

Echoes of Yesterday's Light

In the glow of the sunset, memories beam,
Where laughter intertwines with an old, happy dream.
We pranced through the tales of our youthful parade,
And danced with the echoes of fun that we made.

There once was a picnic that turned into rain,
As sandwiches flew, creating happy mayhem,
From ants in the blanket to bees in the cake,
Those moments of bliss were the bonds that we make.

With ribbons and jokes wrapped around our hearts,
We weathered the seasons, played all the parts.
The stories flow freely, casting shadows so bright,
As we paint with our words in the fading sunlight.

So let's raise a cheer, for the blessings of time,
For the laughter that lingers, the fun in the rhyme.
With cup in our hands and a grin on each face,
Together we travel, through memory's embrace.

Mementos of a Summer Rain

The drips and drops had quite the chase,
A puddle formed, an unexpected race.
We splashed in joy, with socks all wet,
Forgotten worries, the best day yet.

The sun peeked out, a shy little grin,
We giggled loud, let the games begin.
Umbrella flipped, a comical sight,
Spin like a top, oh what a delight!

And mud pies, oh what a fancy feast,
With leaves for plates, we laughed the least.
Each giggle echoed past the lane,
Mementos held through laughter and rain.

As clouds rolled in, we gasped with glee,
When in a storm, we found some tea.
With friendly ghosts in raindrops' song,
Each memory shared, where we belong.

Beneath the Canopy of Dreams

Under the branches, we made our tents,
With wild imaginations and playful intents.
A dragon flew and a knight did roar,
While ants held court on the forest floor.

With berries picked, we filled our bowl,
A feast for kings, or so was our goal.
But bees had plans, they joined the fun,
An uninvited guest, but we still won!

We told ghost tales that made us shriek,
Whispered secrets from cheek to cheek.
As shadows danced, we waved our arms,
Conjuring monsters with their silly charms.

When stars popped out, we made a wish,
For cotton candy and our favorite dish.
But wishes fade with the light of day,
Yet memories stay, and we laugh away.

Recollections in the Dappled Light

Sunbeams flickered, played on our skin,
With laughter spilling, let the fun begin.
A squirrel danced, showing off its flair,
While we hung snacks upon the air.

We built a fortress made of twigs,
With battle cries, we fought off pigs.
Each thud and crash, a battle grand,
Who knew fierce knights could barely stand?

A snack attack took us by surprise,
Bushel of berries, oh what a prize!
We turned our ride to a sugar rush,
Chasing shadows amidst the hush.

As dusk approached, we feigned to bow,
To the monarch of mischief, where we avowed.
But even rulers need a hearty laugh,
To balance kingship with a silly gaffe.

A Symphony of Past Lives

Once there was a summer filled with tune,
Where cicadas played beneath the moon.
We crafted crowns of dandelions,
While giggles soared like sweetest sirens.

Underneath the swing, tales were spun,
Of daring feats and races run.
Each roar of laughter, a thunderous sound,
As time whirred by, yet joy was found.

We'd trade our woes for a spiral slide,
And take our chances on the wild side.
With a spoon and a bowl, all chaos broke,
Inventing smoothies, what a weird joke!

And when the stars found their place in the sky,
We dreamed of gardens where wild trolls fry.
In the symphony of youth's vibrant haze,
We'll find our rhythm through those playful days.

Whispers of Wood and Worn Shoes

A creak in the boards, a ghostly alarm,
As squirrels play tag with my wayward charm.
Old shoes on the steps, they dance with the breeze,
While I shuffle and wonder, do they wear my knees?

The memories giggle, they jump and they sway,
They tease me for stories I've lost on the way.
Each splinter a giggle, each crack a sly grin,
As I trip over memories, my dance begins.

The cat yawns and stretches, an audience found,
With one paw in the air, for the show I surround.
He's judging my moves, with his bright little eyes,
While the old porch keeps laughing beneath sunny skies.

"This step is too high!" I declare with a pout,
But the wood and the shoes just toss laughter about.
And through whispered chuckles, they tell me it's clear,
The funniest moments are those made right here.

Sunlight and Shadows Beneath Old Eaves

Sunlight spills down like a golden surprise,
Shadow dances play tricks, good luck for my eyes.
I'm caught in a battle, with hats made of light,
Where sunlight spills laughter, and shadows take flight.

Old chairs creak softly, a symphony grand,
As I share all my stories with the porch's kind hand.
Each cushion a listener, each beam a dear friend,
While the breeze carries giggles, on this I depend.

A bird lands beside me, he's eyeing my treat,
His chirps turn to chuckles, a salty-sweet greet.
I toss him a crumb, with a wink and a grin,
Together we revel, let the fun times begin.

The sun dips down low, weaving tales in the night,
While shadows exchange secrets, hidden from sight.
With each fading splendor, I know it's quite clear:
The joy of the day lives on, long after cheer.

Echoes of Laughter in Timeless Corners

In the corner, a chair has a story to tell,
Of snickers from children and secrets that dwell.
With cushions well-worn from a summer's bright play,
They cradle the laughter, come what may.

A tomato plant's trying to join in the fun,
But all he can muster is a glance at the sun.
As I snicker at weeds, they wiggle and tease,
A garden of giggles grows strong in the breeze.

The wind chimes are chuckling, a rhythm so fine,
Each jingle a laugh, as stars start to shine.
"Might we join the show?" the fireflies inquire,
With a flicker of light, they dance like a choir.

So here in these corners, with laughter so bright,
Life's memories mingle, and it feels just right.
With echoes and whispers, the night finds its tune,
In this silly embrace beneath the bright moon.

Stories Cradled by Railing and Time

The railing is old, but it's sturdy and true,
It's cradling tales from both me and from you.
Each chip and each scratch has a giggle to share,
As we lean on the stories that linger in air.

A fly buzzes close, with his own little plan,
As I shoo him away, he just laughs, "Yes, I can!"
The railing chuckles, it sways side to side,
A partner in mischief, with stories as guide.

With cups full of lemonade, we watch all the fun,
As kids chase the shadows, in the bright summer sun.
Their giggles resound, as they tumble and race,
Creating a symphony, a sweet joyful space.

Old creaks play along as we sit here and sigh,
For every story whispers a joke in the sky.
With laughter entwined in the twilight's soft grip,
Time dances around us, on this memory trip.

Cherished Words Held Close

In the creaky chair we sit,
Remembering all the silly wit.
The cat's gotten into the pie,
And the dog just let out a sigh.

Old jokes are making a return,
As candles flicker and shadows churn.
Grandma's stories spin and twirl,
With the most unexpected curl.

We laugh till our stomachs ache,
Each memory a delicious cake.
The lost socks and their mad race,
Revisiting each familiar face.

Time is a jester, a true rogue,
With knee-slapping tales and a spoke.
In this cozy space of glee,
Every sigh spills humor like tea.

The Repeat of Fading Cries

Echoes of laughter sweep the floor,
As we reminisce, we crave more.
The ice cream truck that never came,
Oh, the antics we can't quite tame.

With echoes of a playful scream,
Long-lost cousins, like a dream.
Bouncing balls that once flew high,
Now just memories passing by.

Pants that shrank from summer sun,
And shoes that squeaked when we would run.
A slippery slide, a daring fall,
Laughter ringing, memories call.

We weave our tales, let them spin,
Every mishap, a grin within.
Fading cries that bring us cheer,
In tales of yesteryear we steer.

Hummingbirds and Sleepy Eyes

Hummingbirds zoom on by so fast,
While sleepy eyes recall the past.
A garden filled with tasty snacks,
And bees that buzzed with joyful tracks.

Naptime creeping in, oh dear,
The stories morphing, crystal clear.
Dreams of cats in tiny hats,
And giggles shared with acrobats.

Afternoon sun, we bask and grin,
Replaying songs, where to begin?
With tales of clowns and pies that flew,
Oh, recounting days with that crew.

Gentle whispers in the breeze,
Memories dance like buzzing bees.
In every corner, laughter lies,
Underneath those sleepy skies.

The Space Between the Moments

In the gaps where giggles hide,
We find the things we can't confide.
Fumbling socks and missing keys,
Like puzzle pieces lost in trees.

Every pause is filled with cheer,
As echoes of old pranks draw near.
A sneeze that followed the punchline,
Turns our recollections divine.

Between the yawns and gentle sighs,
Are tales of pie fights and silly tries.
The dance of silence sings so loud,
In those moments, we'll be proud.

So come and fill the space with glee,
For laughter will forever be free.
In these memories we find new starts,
The beauty of life, captured in hearts.

Laughter Carried by the Wind

On a chair that creaks and squeaks,
An old cat snoozes, making bizarre squeaks.
A wise old man with tales so tall,
Claims he caught a fish that was bigger than a wall!

The children laugh and run in glee,
Chasing shadows, as wild as can be.
They trip and tumble, oh what a sight,
With giggles that dance like fireflies at night!

Aunt Edna drops her gossip like crumbs,
Spilling secrets of where the wild thing comes.
Her stories twist like pretzel dough,
With plot twists that make us all go, "Whoa!"

Breezes tickle and play at dusk,
There's laughter blooming, in the cozy musk.
We'll remember these moments, so silly, so grand,
With chuckles and chortles, hand in hand.

Embracing the Silent Hours

The sun sets softly, colors in a twist,
Ghosts of laughter linger, they still insist.
Old rocking chairs hum a timeless tune,
As crickets join in, under the moon.

Granddad's corny jokes float in the air,
"Did you hear about the cat with a flair?"
We roll our eyes, then burst into snorts,
While fireflies gather like tiny retorts.

Soft whispers of the past sip lemonade,
With secrets and giggles in the evening shade.
The air is thick with stories told,
Of silly mishaps and pranks we behold.

As night wraps us snug, like a warm quilt,
We cherish the laughter, with joy that we built.
In the stillness, a chuckle invites,
The echoes of joy are the best highlights.

Dusty Footprints of Time

Footprints scatter across the old wood,
Each mark tells a tale, where laughter once stood.
A puppy chased butterflies, round and round,
While the old dog just lay, with wisdom profound.

Ice cream spills, leaving rainbow stains,
On the porch where mischief remains.
A boy climbed too high, in search of the sun,
Only to fall, and laugh while he ran!

We gathered our dreams like fallen leaves,
In the dust of our lives, as sunlight weaves.
The echoes of giggles still fill the air,
With each silly story, wrapped in a prayer.

Memories linger in twilight's embrace,
With shadows of joy, that time can't erase.
So we stomp through the dirt, and dance like kids,
In the footprints of laughter where happiness lives.

Nostalgic Serenades at Sunset

At sunset's glow, we gather near,
With old guitars and songs to cheer.
Silly verses dance on the breeze,
As crickets join with their nighttime tease.

A wise old owl hoots a tune,
While Grandma hums, over a cup of prune.
The tales weave in with harmonized glee,
Of days gone by, wild and free.

We reminisce about the pie fight,
When everyone's face was a glorious sight.
With flour and sugar, mayhem arose,
And the joys of our laughter still comes and goes!

As stars twinkle down, with laughter that shines,
We hold the memories like unwritten lines.
In moments of joy, we find the spark,
As we serenade softly, till it gets dark.

Heartbeats in the Night

In the stillness, crickets sing,
Echoes dance, like forgotten dreams.
Laughter bubbles from lazy lips,
The moon winks at our goofy schemes.

A cat strolls by, acting so wise,
Stealing the show with its sly disguise.
We trip on thoughts, then burst in glee,
As shadows listen, they nod with surprise.

Socks mismatched by a surrounding gnomes,
Every joke spun like a golden comb.
What's better than mishaps shared at dusk?
Each heartbeat adds to our laughter's home.

These nights tucked in mischief's embrace,
Where every tickle's a cherished chase.
Our joy, a pot of brewed delight,
Spiced with memories that time can't erase.

Dividing Glasses and Shared Toasts

Raise your glass, splash of cheer,
A toast to the clumsiness brought near.
Sips that spill and then we giggle,
What's humor without a hilarious wiggle?

A misfit crew with mismatched cups,
Swapping stories of fallen pups.
From quirky dreams to silly fights,
Hand me the vinegar, watch it erupt!

We speak in rhymes, but stumble in time,
Sipping on punch that's aged like a crime.
The bubbles tickle, laughter flows wide,
As we wobble together, a jolly ride.

In this moment, the silliness shines,
Crafted from laughter, these tangled lines.
Our hearts lift with every clink we make,
Bonded forever by joy we can take.

Glimmers of Joy

Glances exchanged, a light in the air,
Chasing shadows, no room for despair.
Lollipops melting on summer days,
We dance with joys in the quirkiest ways.

Sunshine streams through the chaos we dwell,
Tickling our fancies, ringing a bell.
With each little slip, we find a new way,
To laugh at the mess of our everyday play.

Bubbles floating in lemonade cups,
Giggling at thoughts of upside-down pups.
Glimmers of joy in the simplest acts,
We savor these moments, weeks for the facts.

Kites that tangle in a tree's embrace,
Chasing each other with powder-puff grace.
In every giggle, in every fun card,
We stitch our stories, life's vibrant shard.

Fragments of Grief

Memories flicker like shadows at play,
We share the smiles, the tears on display.
A whoopee cushion mistakenly set,
Unexpected giggles, a laugh we won't forget.

Beneath the weight of moments we hold,
Stories unfold, both tender and bold.
A banana peel lies in wait for a foot,
Reminding us all, life's comedic pursuit.

Grinning through stumbles and heartbreak within,
The fragments we cherish dance under our skin.
Pies in the face, a play-dough surprise,
In laughter, we find our way to the skies.

Tears mingle with laughter, a bittersweet treat,
Finding joy in the journey, no small feat.
In shared silly moments, there's comfort in pain,
We lighten the load, again and again.

The Unwritten Stories of Old Wood

Old wood creaks with tales yet told,
Of teenagers sneaking out, feeling bold.
A swing set forgotten, paint peeling away,
Whispers of laughter where children would play.

Beneath the branches, dreams once flew high,
A tea party held under the old blue sky.
Sipping on sunshine, eating make-believe,
The stories of yesteryear, we weave and retrieve.

Sticks that once formed forts fit for kings,
Dancing shadows join in the joy that springs.
In every knot, there's a giggle or two,
Of silly secrets shared by a whimsical crew.

These fragments linger like a sweet little song,
Echoing gently where we all belong.
The old wood chuckles as time passes by,
Reminding us softly to never say bye.

Doors to the Heart's Archive

In dusty corners, secrets hide,
A cat named Whiskers, full of pride.
He guards the tales of days gone by,
And rolls his eyes at every sigh.

Old shoes stacked high on polished shelves,
Memories whisper, 'Be yourself!'
A sock with holes, a broken toy,
Remind us all of simple joy.

The ice cream truck that rings the bell,
With sticky hands, we'd cast our spell.
Chasing dreams on summer nights,
And laughing past the moon's soft lights.

So here we stand, with hearts wide open,
Among the relics, unbroken token.
Each door we close holds laughter's echo,
In this place, we're never let go.

The Dance of Light and Shade

Sunlight dances through the trees,
With shadows wagging in the breeze.
We twirl in circles, round and round,
As laughter sets our spirits bound.

The garden gnomes nod in delight,
As we leap into the fading light.
A bird gets jealous, starts to sing,
While crickets chirp and crickets cling.

We stumble over flower beds,
Get tangled up in silly threads.
Whispers of twilight start to play,
As giggles sweep the night away.

We trip and laugh, a lovely mess,
In the cool night air, we feel no stress.
We dance between the light and shade,
In this symphony, memories laid.

Heartstrings in the Evening Chill

On rocking chairs, we sway and hum,
Our minds alight with tales so fun.
The evening chill tugs at our toes,
And wraps us close in faded prose.

With hot cocoa mugs and marshmallows,
We sit and chat, like best of fellows.
Grandpa's stories weave a thread,
Of quirky ducks and a lucky spread.

A squirrel leaps, with nuts in tow,
His acrobatics steal the show.
We laugh until our bellies ache,
At how he slips, makes such a quake.

Under the moon's warm, shining hand,
We gather dreams like grains of sand.
In heartstrings tight, we're woven still,
Memories dance, a grand goodwill.

Tick Tocks from a Wooden Swing

The swing creaks soft, a gentle song,
As we rock back and forth, not long.
Counting clouds that sail on high,
While giggles chase the birds that fly.

A simple game of 'Who can swing higher?'
Two kids dream big, hearts on fire.
With each push, our laughter sprawls,
Tick tocks echo, fun-filled calls.

Sticky fingers, popsicle goo,
Shiny wrappers, red and blue.
Cousins race, who's the fastest yet?
Whispers echo, a no-regret bet.

As dusk unfurls its blanket wide,
We chat about the stars we've spied.
From that swing, our dreams take flight,
In our hearts, we'll hold the night.

Nostalgia Draped in Morning Dew

In the early light we'd dance,
Barefoot antics, a merry prance.
Sticky fingers from last night's snack,
Oh, how we'd plot to sneak it back.

Silly hats and mismatched socks,
Building forts with all the blocks.
Lemonade spills on the old rug,
We'd laugh and hug like a big bug.

In every crease, a joke we'd find,
With sunshine painting joy in kind.
Hiding laughter behind the door,
Our innocent giggles, we'd want more.

A world of mischief through these eyes,
Where every glance, a sweet surprise.
Though years have passed, the moments stay,
In morning dew, they softly play.

Chasing Fireflies and Whispered Secrets

Underneath the moon's soft glow,
We'd chase the sparkles, high and low.
Daring each other to catch a few,
Flickering lights, a summer view.

Whispers floated on the breeze,
Telling secrets with silly ease.
Making up tales of pirates bold,
With treasure maps and a world of gold.

In the tall grass, we'd tumble about,
Trying hard to stifle a shout.
Each firefly caught was a badge of cheer,
Our laughter echoing, loud and clear.

As night wore on, we'd draw the lines,
Imagining futures as big as pines.
Even now, the glow seems true,
A dance of memories from me to you.

Crickets Sing of What Once Was

Crickets chirp, a tune so sweet,
Reminding us of our little feet.
Recalling summers, both hot and bright,
Where mischief ruled the balmy nights.

We'd sneak out past the fence so tall,
Straying far from the evening call.
Stolen cookies and forgotten rules,
Chased by the laughter of our old-school fools.

In every croak, a story's spun,
Of daring deeds under the sun.
We journeyed worlds on wooden swings,
Of imaginary kings and silly things.

As shadows fall and the stars appear,
The crickets sing, we still can hear.
For in those sounds, we find our bliss,
A song of youth, we can't dismiss.

Welcoming Storms to Forgotten Tales

Raindrops drumming on a tin roof,
Call us back to the mischievous proof.
With blankets pulled and torches high,
We'd weave our tales as the thunder cried.

Tent forts built with chairs and sheets,
Having feasts of imaginary treats.
Each crack of lightning, a laugh in fright,
As we spun yarns till the morning light.

Soggy socks and muddy shoes,
A dance of joy, we could not lose.
With every storm, adventure drew,
In mischief and giggles, we all flew.

Those tales have weathered through the years,
Bringing back laughter and happy tears.
We'd open our hearts to the tempest's wail,
For storms would come to our silly tale.

www.ingramcontent.com/pod-product-compliance
Lightning Source LLC
Chambersburg PA
CBHW070305120526
44590CB00017B/2566